Lindow Man
Jody Joy

THE BRITISH MUSEUM PRESS

that the body was ancient. On 17 August it was shown by
radiocarbon dating to be at least 1,000 years old. Meanwhile
the landowners had presented the remains to the British
Museum and by 21 August they were taken to London. The
remains were stored initially at the mortuary of the Middlesex
Hospital until a team of experts had been assembled to
assist Museum staff in a planned scientific investigation,
and a suitable space at a British Museum storage facility,
Franks House in East London, had been made ready.

On 24 September the remains were taken to Franks
House and the process of removing peat from the body
began. This was a slow and laborious task as the body had to
be kept at a temperature of below 4°C to prevent the onset of
decay. Excavation time was restricted as the body had to be
returned to a refrigeration unit every time it rose above that
temperature. The peat was removed using various wooden
and plastic implements, by hand and using jets of water. The
excavators started near the exposed flap of skin discovered
by Turner and worked away from that point. To aid the
process X-rays were taken at the Middlesex Hospital,
through which it was possible to identify an arm, backbone
and ribs and a skull; however, the images were not very clear
because of the mass of peat surrounding the body. At this
stage the body was lying on its back (it had been turned over

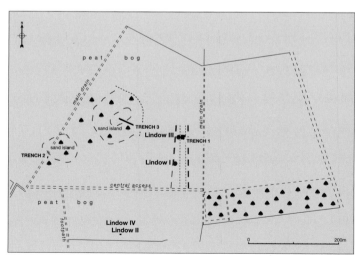

4 Lifting the section of peat containing the remains of Lindow Man on to a plywood sheet.

5 The body emerges
from the peat.

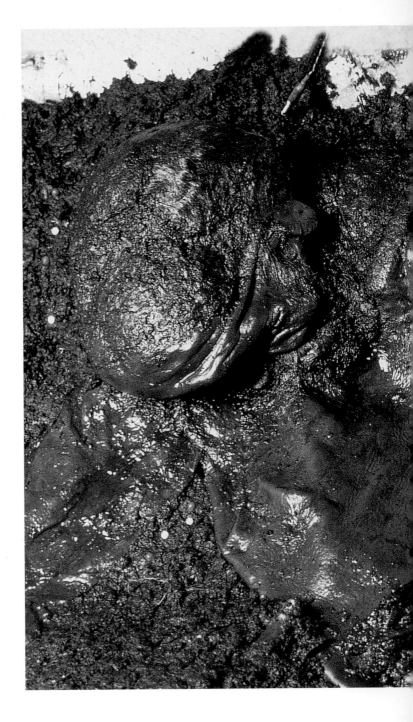

6 *right* Cartoon which appeared in the *Sunday Telegraph* on 7 October 1984. The leader of the opposition at the time, Neil Kinnock, is depicted in the guise of Lindow Man. He is viewed by his Front Bench colleagues.

7 *opposite, top* Filming for the QED documentary at Lindow Moss.

8 *opposite, bottom* Fox-fur armband on Lindow Man's left arm.

since its discovery) and the investigation continued until the whole of the front had been exposed. It was then cleaned and recorded. The body was turned over and the same technique was undertaken to remove the peat from the back.

Only after all the peat had been removed could the full extent of preservation be appreciated. The remains comprised the well-preserved upper torso of an adult male. He was well muscled, his hair and beard were present, and it was possible to make out clear facial features such as a furrowed brow. He was naked except for a fox-fur armband on his upper left arm. Around his neck was a twisted cord of animal sinew, and on the top of his head and around his neck there were signs of physical trauma.

The process of uncovering the body took five days and was filmed for a BBC 'QED' documentary. When it was screened in April 1985, the film was watched by more than 10 million people. In the second week of the investigation the discovery was announced to the press and received worldwide attention. The body was called 'Pete Marsh' by journalists; the scientists preferred the name 'Lindow Man'. Over twenty years later Lindow Man's appeal continues. Visitors to the Museum are fascinated by the remarkable preservation of his body, and he has become a prehistoric celebrity, appearing in numerous television documentaries.

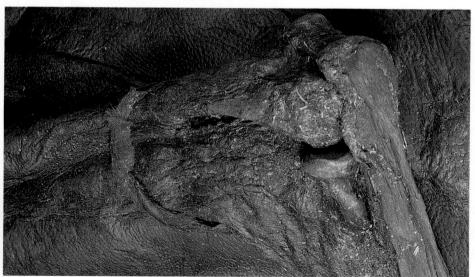

13

9 View of Lindow Man
taken from above his
current display case.

Chapter 2
Murder on the Moss

The body of Lindow Man is not the only human remains to have been discovered at Lindow Moss. During the 1980s workmen at the peat-cutting company uncovered well-preserved ancient human remains on five separate occasions and the remains of at least three, possibly four, bodies have been found there.

The first discovery at Lindow Moss was made on 13 May 1983, a year before that of Lindow Man, on the elevator at the company depot. While removing objects that could damage the shredding mill through which the peat was processed, Andy Mould and Stephen Dooley spotted a round object, 20 cm in diameter, which intrigued them. They joked that it could be a dinosaur egg, but after they hosed it down it became clear it was a human skull. The site manager, Ken Harewood, immediately took the skull to the police. It was that of a woman aged between thirty and fifty years old. Her left eyeball was still in place, along with some of her hair, but identifying features such as the cheek- and jawbones were missing.

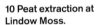

10 Peat extraction at Lindow Moss.

A murder investigation

The Macclesfield Police were extremely interested by the discovery of the skull because at that time they were investigating an unsolved murder. During a police interview two suspects of another crime had told of a previous cellmate who boasted of murdering his wife. Peter Reyn-Bardt claimed that he had disposed of his wife Malika twenty years earlier, in 1960, by dismembering and burning her remains in his garden. Reyn-Bardt's property at that time backed on to Lindow Moss. The skull was found just 300 metres away from the Reyn-Bardt house.

When first interviewed by the police in January 1983 Reyn-Bardt firmly denied murdering his wife, and investigation of the garden produced no evidence. However, when informed of the discovery of the skull, Reyn-Bardt made a full confession. Suspicious of the skull's age, the police consulted archaeologists, who radiocarbon-dated a sample taken from it. The date obtained showed that the skull was around 1,800 years old, proving that the woman was alive when the Romans occupied Britain, and therefore was not connected with the police murder inquiry! Despite this, Reyn-Bardt was convicted of the murder of his wife in December 1983 on the strength of his own confession.

11 The company elevator.

17

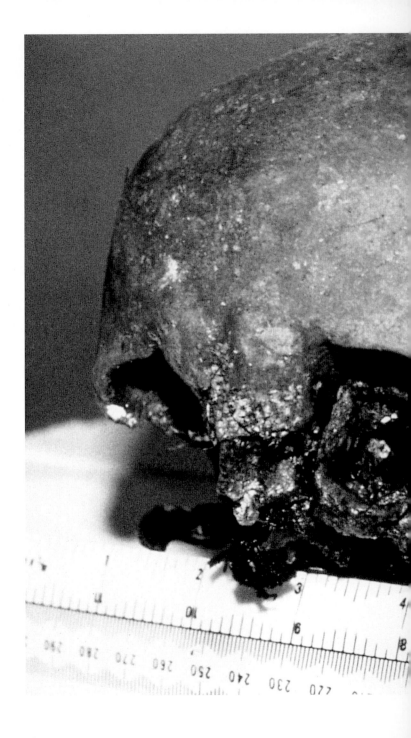

12 A woman's skull found at Lindow Moss, now known as 'Lindow I'.

Further discoveries

Even though the site was periodically monitored by the Cheshire county archaeologist, Rick Turner, there were no further discoveries at Lindow Moss until 1987.

On 6 February that year, part of another body was exposed, again by the men working on the site elevator. Happy that the remains were most probably ancient, the police left the investigation of this body to the archaeologists. The next day all the recently excavated peat was sorted and over seventy different pieces of the body were uncovered. Although survival of bone was poor, the condition of the tissue was better than that of Lindow Man. The total remains consisted of the back of an adult male, a hand and a leg. An archaeological investigation of the Moss, funded by English Heritage, established the likely original location of the body, which was probably broken up when the peat was excavated and processed. Further discoveries were made at Lindow Moss on 14 June and 12 September 1988, when parts of the buttocks, left leg and right thigh of an adult male were uncovered. As these discoveries were made only 15 metres from where Lindow Man was found, they are probably missing pieces from his body. Future DNA analysis may mean we can prove this conclusively.

What is a bog body?

The remains from Lindow Moss belong to a well-known group of discoveries known as 'bog bodies', a term that describes any human remains found in a bog (an area of wet, spongy ground). When bog plants, particularly mosses, decay they form peat. Bog bodies have been recovered across lowland north-west Europe, specifically Britain, Ireland, Denmark, the Netherlands and north-west Germany. Some bog bodies are nearly 6,000 years old, others only a few hundred years old. Bodies are found in bogs for various reasons. Some are deliberate burials, others may have been the victims of accidental drowning. It is impossible to determine exactly how many bog bodies from these countries have been uncovered, but it is possibly up to 2,000. Many were discovered hundreds of years ago and then reburied, so we only have documentary evidence to prove they existed.

In the British Isles human remains recovered from bogs have been recorded since the seventeenth century. 106 cases have been reported in England and Wales and 35 in Scotland, some at least as well preserved as Lindow Man. Unfortunately when many of these remains were uncovered there was no way to preserve them. Many were reburied soon after discovery as they had begun to decompose outside the bog. Peat covers 5.8 per cent of the British landscape, but rates of peat loss have been dramatic. Lindow Moss once extended over 600 hectares, but owing to peat extraction and land drainage it has now been reduced to under a tenth of that size. Over 96 per cent of Britain's raised bogs have been lost since 1850, which may explain why the bulk of bog body discoveries were made after that date.

Of particular interest was the discovery in 1958 of a human head in Worsley Moss, just 20 kilometres from Lindow Moss. It belonged to a man aged between twenty and thirty years old when he died. Worsley Man, as he became known, died some time in the Roman period. In addition to decapitation, he received injuries sufficient to fracture his skull and, like Lindow Man, had a cord tied around his neck.

When did Lindow Man die?

The term 'bog body' usually refers to human remains dating from 500 BC to AD 100. This period is known as the Iron Age because people first used iron to make tools and weapons. They lived on farms or in small settlements, harvested crops such as wheat, barley and rye, and reared cattle, sheep and pigs. The Iron Age is perhaps best known for its elaborate artefacts, such as torcs and display shields, made from bronze and precious metals, which are popularly known as Celtic Art. In some regions people built large settlements with huge earth ramparts, known as hillforts. These extraordinary artefacts and sites provide tantalizing clues to the nature of life in the Iron Age but it remains a mysterious period from the European past. Water was significant to Iron Age people. Metal objects, particularly weapons, were deliberately placed in rivers and lakes, possibly as offerings to the gods. Bog people similarly

13 The Battersea
Shield, an Iron Age
artefact found in the
River Thames at
Battersea Bridge,
London.

may have been placed in their watery locations as offerings to the gods, the victims of ritual sacrifice.

The technique of radiocarbon dating, which measures the rate of decay of a radioactive form of carbon found in all living organisms, known as carbon 14, was used to date the human remains from Lindow Moss. All dated remains are from the late Iron Age and early Roman periods (see the table below).

To date Lindow Man, twenty-four different samples were taken from several parts of his body and the peat that surrounded him. Disagreement between the dates obtained by two different laboratories led Ian Stead, the British Museum curator in charge of the scientific investigation, to favour dates obtained from the peat, which was securely dated to the Iron Age. However, further testing and reconciliation of existing dates shows that Lindow Man died some time in the first century AD (2 BC–AD 119). This date is intriguing as it raises the question of whether Lindow Man died in the Iron Age or some time after the Roman conquest of northern England in the early AD 60s.

Towards the end of the first century BC and later, some regions where bog bodies have been found were conquered by the Romans. The Romans worshipped many different gods and often built shrines in locations such as springs, which were significant to Iron Age people. Roman law prohibited human sacrifice, so if Lindow Man did die after the Roman conquest then the circumstances of his death may have to be reinterpreted.

The discoveries from Lindow Moss

Number	Date of discovery	Description	Date
Lindow I	13 May 1983	Head of a woman	AD 90–440
Lindow II	1 August 1984	Torso and left leg of a man, known as Lindow Man	2 BC–AD 129
Lindow III	6 February 1987	Many pieces of an adult male	AD 30–225
Lindow IV	14 June and 12 September 1988	Buttocks, left leg and right thigh of an adult man. Possibly further remains of Lindow II (Lindow Man)	

Chapter 3
Investigating and conserving a bog body

During October and November 1984 Lindow Man was examined by a series of specialists. Only twenty bog bodies so far discovered are as well preserved as Lindow Man and fewer still have been the subject of such a thorough scientific investigation. Owing to their excellent state of preservation, bog bodies offer a unique insight into life in past communities and scientific research has enabled us to piece together the circumstances of Lindow Man's death; the contents of his last meal; to establish how old he was when he died; his state of health; and to reveal his facial features. Examination of the peat that immediately surrounded him has also allowed us to reconstruct the environment of Lindow Moss 2,000 years ago.

On the move
A medical investigation of Lindow Man's body was initially undertaken using various non-invasive techniques. This involved his remains taking a tour of many of London's major medical institutions. X-rays were taken at the Middlesex Hospital. Xeroradiography, a type of dry X-ray made on paper rather than film, was conducted at the Royal Marsden Hospital. This technique has been used successfully to examine Egyptian mummies, and revealed Lindow Man to have a number of internal injuries, a broken rib and fragments of skull inside his cranial cavity. Computer Tomography (CT) scanning at St Bartholomew's

14 Xeroradiograph of the top of Lindow Man's skull, clearly showing a fragment of bone in his cranial cavity.

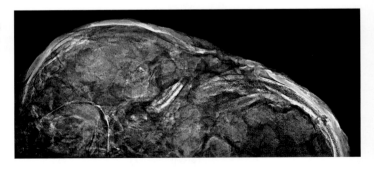

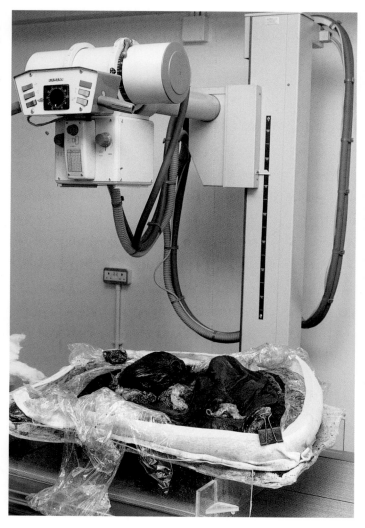

15 Lindow Man being xeroradiographed at the Royal Marsden Hospital.

Hospital provided a complete picture of Lindow Man's remains, showing clear images of his skull and vertebrae, and clearly identified a broken neck and skull fractures. At Picker International Ltd in Wembley, manufacturers of magnetic resonance imaging (MRI) machines, the most up-to-date machine was made available to scientists, producing excellent images of the brain inside the cranial cavity.

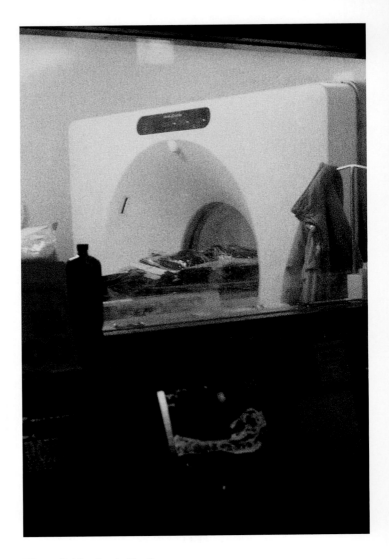

16 Lindow Man inside
a CT scanner at
St Bartholomew's
Hospital.

What did he look like?
Although not all of Lindow Man's body was recovered
intact, based on the length of his leg- and arm bones it
has been calculated that he was between 5 feet 6 inches
and 5 feet 8 inches tall. This is shorter than the modern
average for an adult male but measurements of Iron Age
skeletons show that he was slightly taller than average for
that period. Based on his height and well-built stature,

Lindow Man probably weighed around 10 stone. Different bones fuse at different ages after that particular part of the body has stopped growing. By comparing when these different stages in the life cycle take place in modern populations we can calculate the age at death of ancient people. Xeroradiographs of Lindow Man show that his clavicle bone had only recently fused, meaning that he was probably around twenty-five years old when he died. Attempts have even been made to reconstruct what Lindow Man looked like. Richard Neave of Manchester University modelled a copy of Lindow Man's skull using radiographs and produced a facial reconstruction. This was the first time the method had been used on a bog body. The facial reconstruction produced by Neave appears very lifelike, although it is not certain how accurate it is.

Microscopic analyses of Lindow Man's hair and nails revealed that he was well groomed. His hair was quite short, ranging from 1 to 9 cm in length. The longest hair was at the neck, providing the overall effect of a well-styled mullet! Although his hair is now red, this was caused by chemicals in the bog and we think it was originally dark brown. Notches at the end of the hairs on his face are characteristic of the use of shears, which were used to roughly trim his beard and moustache. Shears are often found on later Iron Age and Roman period sites. They vary in size and although larger shears were probably used on livestock, smaller versions were used to trim human hair. A green fluorescence was observed in Lindow Man's hair and the fox-fur armband. Combined with evidence for high levels of copper found on the skin of the remains of Lindow III, it has been argued that these residues indicate pigments which were used to paint the human body. This was a practice observed by Romans writing about Iron Age peoples. However, scientific analysis of these residues showed that they are caused in bogs when organic remains are exposed to acid in the absence of oxygen.

Lindow Man filed his nails. The surfaces of his fingernails retain a smooth appearance even at 1,000X magnification. When compared to the surface of modern-day fingernails they most closely resembled those of a

17 *left* Facial reconstruction of how Lindow Man may have looked.

18 *right* The reconstruction of Lindow Man's head getting a final touch-up before being placed on display.

female manicurist. Toilet sets, including tweezers and 'ear scoops' (used to remove ear wax), are found in the later Iron Age and Roman periods. Physical appearance is a powerful means of communicating social identity, and people during the later Iron Age altered the way they looked in order to express social status. Perhaps Lindow Man was an individual of relatively high standing in society. Certainly there were few signs of surface damage on his nails, indicating that he had not performed any hard manual labour, such as farming activities, in the months leading up to his death.

What was his last meal?

Examination of Lindow Man's internal organs revealed that part of his stomach and small intestine had been preserved, offering the exciting possibility of discovering the contents of his last meal and providing extremely useful information about ancient diet and farming methods. Samples of the gut contents were analysed by a number of different specialists. They revealed that on the day or the day before he died, Lindow Man ate a meal consisting of finely ground wheat and barley. In addition, weed seeds commonly associated with arable cultivation were discovered. It was not possible to determine whether the wheat and barley were part of the same meal but analysis of the wheat shows that it was heated to 200–250°C. Unlike some other European bog

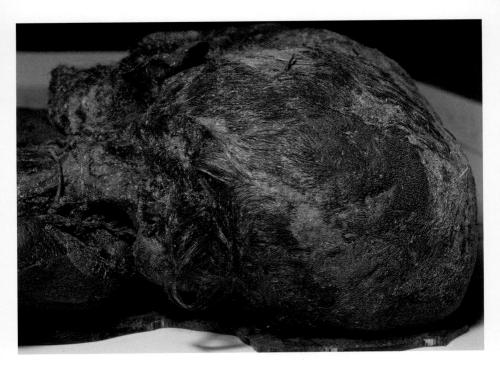

bodies, Lindow Man's last meal was not boiled gruel; it was cooked at a much higher temperature and was probably a flat unleavened griddle cake, heated over an open fire.

Shortly before Lindow III died he ate hazelnuts, as well as wheat and rye. Old Croghan Man, recently discovered in Ireland, ate a meal of milk and cereal. Grauballe Man, found in Denmark in the 1950s, ate a gruel made of weed seeds, which were a by-product from the processing and cleaning of cereals. This highly nutritious – although probably not very tasty – food was similar to the final meal of Tollund Man, also from Denmark.

Much has been made of the mistletoe pollen found in Lindow Man's gut. This is seen as significant by some authors because the Roman historian Pliny wrote that mistletoe was used in ceremonies by a priestly class of people known as the druids. Only four grains of mistletoe pollen were discovered in Lindow Man's gut. The mistletoe may have been taken as part of a special food, drink or medicine. It is also possible, as only a small quantity has been discovered, that the mistletoe could have been ingested inadvertently. Contrary to many interpretations that have sought to show that the last meals of other bog bodies were ritually significant, the actual evidence is more mundane. The final meals of Grauballe Man and Tollund Man are unlikely to have been regarded as 'fine dining' in prehistoric Denmark. Lindow Man and Lindow III did not eat agricultural by-products but their last meals were still relatively simple. Until recently the presence of ergot (*claviceps purpurea*) – a parasitic fungus that infects cereals – in Grauballe Man's last meal was thought to be highly significant. Ergot can produce LSD-like hallucinogenic effects as it causes blood vessels to contract, restricting the flow of blood to the brain. It was thought that ergot was deliberately included in Grauballe Man's last meal as part of a ceremony associated with his death. However, recent research has shown the level of ergot in his last meal to be within current EU guidelines and unlikely to have caused greater hallucinatory effects than bread found in any supermarket!

Future scientific analysis of Lindow Man's hair could tell us what kinds of food he ate in the weeks and months leading up to his death. This would help to determine the season in which he died, as different foods are available at different times of the year. This kind of research will only be possible if human remains are stored securely by museums, and their condition regularly monitored by museum staff.

The contents of Lindow Man's last meal and the peat that surrounded him also provide evidence of an intensification of agricultural production in the region around the time of his death. Analysis of pollen in the layer of peat in which Lindow Man's body was found shows that some time in the late first century BC there was a major phase of deforestation in the immediate vicinity of Lindow Moss. Land was cleared for agriculture and cereals such as wheat, barley and oats were cultivated. Lindow Man's stomach contained fine sand or grit, also found in the stomachs of Egyptian mummies and Danish bog bodies, which is evidence of the use of grinding stones called querns in the processing of grain to produce flour.

Some unwanted parasites

Lindow Man, a well-built man in the prime of his life, was in good health when he died. He had mild arthritis in his lower spine, although this is common in skeletons from the pre-modern period. Eggs from intestinal parasites were found in his small intestine. They were from two species of worm: whipworm and maw worm. Parasitic worms live in the lower intestine and were widespread among people in Europe before the development of adequate sewerage systems. Acute infestations of whipworm can cause poor appetite, diarrhoea and sometimes mild intestinal bleeding. Infestation of humans by maw worms, which can grow up to 30 cm long, is linked to the domestication of the pig, which carries the parasite. Occasionally the maw worm causes lung disease and intestinal blockage, but it is more likely to bring about discomfort, diarrhoea and nausea. We do not know how badly Lindow Man was infected by worms; most likely they caused him only minor discomfort. Parasitic worm eggs have been discovered in other bog bodies such as Lindow III, Grauballe Man and Tollund Man, and these kinds of infections were probably widespread throughout the human populations of Iron Age Europe.

Why are human remains found in bogs so well preserved?

Natural processes of decay can be rapid. Under certain conditions a dead human body will be unrecognizable within a few days. Occasionally, however, some natural processes will conserve a body. For example, burial in sand can quickly dry out a corpse, significantly slowing down the rate of decay. Human bodies can also be preserved in peat bogs: here skin and hair are very often well preserved but bones fair less well. There are several reasons why preservation occurs in bogs. They are often cold, acidic and lack oxygen, making them relatively hostile environments for putrefactive micro-organisms. Sphagnum mosses also have an important effect. They grow in raised or 'blanket' bogs, in which all of the best-preserved bog bodies have been found. When sphagnum mosses die they release a kind

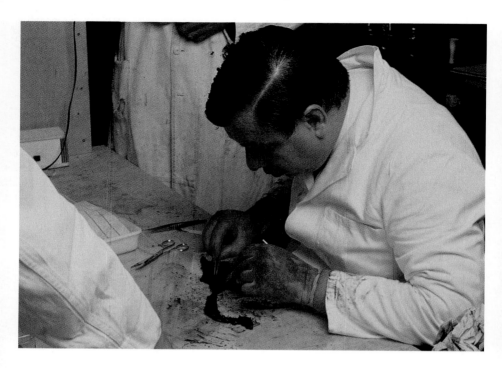

of sugar called sphagnan, which acts as a natural tanning
agent, effectively turning animal and human skin, tendons,
ligaments and muscle into leather. Sphagnan also reacts
with the digestive enzymes produced by decay-causing
bacteria, acting to immobilize them near the surface of the
peat. It makes the skin of bog bodies turn brown and hair
turn red.

Conserving Lindow Man's body

During the scientific investigation Lindow Man's body
began to decay and a suitable method of conserving it had
to be devised. This brought up the issue of exactly how one
conserves a waterlogged human body to ensure that it
survives intact into the future without drying out. The
Conservation Department at the British Museum has
considerable expertise in preserving waterlogged wood
and leather from archaeological sites, but this was the first
time it had needed to tackle a bog body. The scientist in
charge of Lindow Man's conservation, Sherif Omar, visited

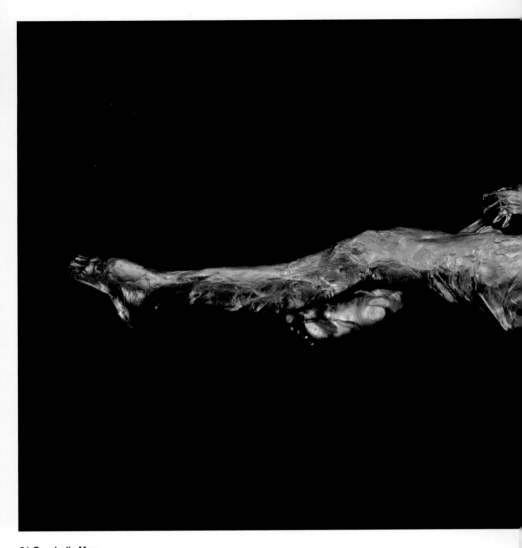

21 Grauballe Man,
found near the present-
day village of Grauballe
in Central Jutland,
Denmark, in 1952.

a number of European museums in which bog bodies had been conserved. The head of Tollund Man, in the Silkeborg Museum, Denmark, was treated with alcohol to drive out water, and then with paraffin to replace the alcohol. In the Moesgård Museum in Denmark, Grauballe Man was conserved by finishing the tanning process that had already begun in the bog. Oak bark was used as a tanning agent and the body was immersed in a solution of oak bark and water for eighteen months. To prevent the body from drying out it was then immersed in a solution of Turkish red oil. Although some fantastic results had been obtained using various methods, none of the museum conservators visited by Omar was satisfied with existing treatments. For example, although the results of the conservation of the head of Tollund Man are aesthetically pleasing, it is estimated to have shrunk by 12–14 per cent. On this basis it was decided that an alternative process, freeze-drying, may produce better results.

From the 1970s onwards, freeze-drying had been used routinely to conserve waterlogged material and was especially advantageous because it reduces shrinkage. The process removes water from organic remains by sublimation, turning the water contained within into ice and converting the ice into a vapour, which is then removed. The vapour from sublimation can be seen when one takes an ice cream from a shop freezer on a hot summer's day. Removing moisture from organic remains prevents bacteria and other agents of decay from living and reproducing and allows the remains to be stored indefinitely in ambient conditions. Freeze-drying is preferred over air-drying because much of the structure of the remains is preserved, which acts to reduce shrinkage. When a sample of Lindow Man's skin was air-dried it shrank by up to 50 per cent, and became hard and brittle. Shrinkage is also reduced when freeze-drying is combined with a pre-treatment with a consolidant such as polyethylene glycol (PEG), which is available in a number of different forms. Before this pre-treatment was undertaken, a number of experiments were carried out using pigskin, chosen because of its resemblance to human skin, to determine which solution of PEG would produce the best results.

Lindow Man was immersed in a solution of PEG 400 and distilled water for ten weeks. He was then wrapped in cling film and frozen at a temperature of -26°C for three days. At the Ancient Monuments Laboratory he was freeze-dried for four weeks. Initial measurements suggested that the freeze-drying was successful: shrinkage of the body was less than 5 per cent and, although it had become less flexible, it could still be handled easily. There was a noticeable lightening of skin colour, and lighter and darker areas on the skin surface mirrored the folds of the cling film in which he was wrapped. There was no distinguishable smell coming from the body. Over twenty years on, Lindow Man is still in good condition. He is kept in an environmentally controlled display case, which maintains temperature to within 1° of 20°C and relative humidity to within 2 per cent of 55 per cent. The intensity of light in his display case is now carefully monitored, as it was discovered that previous exposure to strong light had caused his skin to lighten over the years.

40

22 Injuries to the top of
Lindow Man's head.

Examination of the body also revealed a possible wound on the right side of the neck and a narrow opening about 3 cm long on the right collar bone. The edges of the wound to the right side of the neck were cleanly cut, perhaps indicating that it was caused by an incision from a sharp-edged weapon such as a knife. The possible wound on the right side of the chest cannot be confirmed as the skin in this area of the body is decayed. Therefore this flaw in his skin could be the result of decomposition rather than a stab wound.

Xeroradiographs show that Lindow Man has a fracture to the eighth or ninth left posterior rib. A fracture of the spine was also discovered in the neck and his head was twisted to the right at the point of the break; this explains the awkward position of the head when Lindow Man was first discovered.

The events leading to death

Iain West provided a potential interpretation to explain Lindow Man's injuries and the possible sequence of actions leading to his death. According to West, Lindow Man was struck on the top of his head twice with a heavy object, perhaps a narrow-bladed axe. These injuries were delivered while he was standing or kneeling and he was struck from behind. The broken rib occurred at about the time of death, caused by a heavy blow to the back of the chest. The animal sinew found at Lindow Man's neck was then used as a garrotte. A stick or piece of metal was inserted into the loop of the sinew and was twisted until he was strangled, causing the neck fracture and marks on the front and sides of Lindow Man's neck. Then a deep cut was made at the side of the neck, which severed the jugular vein. The garrotte acted to quicken the flow of blood from the neck. The final act was to place Lindow Man face down in a pool in the bog. This is the account of Lindow Man's death that has been presented for many years beside the exhibit in the British Museum.

However, this interpretation of the evidence is open to debate. Robert Connolly, a lecturer in physical anthropology at the University of Liverpool, also examined Lindow Man's remains, and presented an alternative explanation of his injuries. Connolly agreed with West that the wound to the top of Lindow Man's head was delivered using a blunt-edged instrument and would have rendered him unconscious but was not immediately fatal. But unlike West, Connolly believed that Lindow Man's neck was not broken by the animal sinew being used as a garrotte but rather by a blow to the back of the head. Following this interpretation, Lindow Man died as a result of a series of vicious blows to the top and back of his head. Connolly suggested that the sinew was not a garrotte, but instead secured some kind of neck ornament. Ligature marks around the neck were caused by the sinew as the body bloated when it was submerged in the pool. All other possible injuries identified by West are explained by Connolly as changes to the body occurring after death. The rib fracture could have happened some time after death, perhaps when Lindow Man was recovered. The possible wound to the right side of the neck could be the result of tearing and stresses caused by changes to the body after it entered the bog.

The function of the animal sinew and the possible stab wound to the neck are the main points of contention between these two interpretations of how Lindow Man died. They are still a cause of debate. If the sinew was used to secure a necklace or other ornament, it would have been extremely tight-fitting. On the other hand, analysis of the knot in the sinew revealed that, although the knot is relatively simple, its ends are neatly cut. If the sinew was just intended for execution, why take so much care to neaten it? Alternative explanations of the presence of the sinew around Lindow Man's neck can also be put forward. For example, rather than functioning as a garrotte or a necklace, the sinew could have been used as a tether to prevent his escape.

Like Connolly, West originally thought the possible wound to the right side of Lindow Man's neck was the result of the skin stretching and splitting after he was placed in the bog. But on further examination West thought that the straight edges of the split in the skin indicated that it was caused by a sharp-edged instrument such as a knife. It is impossible to be sure about this injury; certainly if it was a cut to the throat it was not as violent as the injury inflicted on Grauballe Man, whose throat was cut from ear to ear.

Debate about the events leading to Lindow Man's death is likely to continue and it is hoped that future scientific examination will shed further light on this discussion. We know that Lindow Man was hit on the top of the head twice with an object such as a blunt-edged axe. Although these injuries were not immediately fatal they rendered him unconscious. The neck fracture was the fatal injury but we do not know whether it was caused by the sinew found around his neck being used as a garrotte, or by further blows to the back of the head. What we can be certain about is that his death was violent. It can even be described as 'overkill', as much more force was used than was necessary to kill him.

Robbery and murder versus ritual sacrifice

From the physical evidence it is possible to establish the sequence of events that led to Lindow Man's death, although there is some disagreement about the details. However, this evidence does not on its own explain why he was killed. Combined with archaeological and textual evidence, it has led to different interpretations explaining why Lindow Man died.

Robert Connolly thought that he could have died during combat or after a violent robbery. Because he was naked when he was found and no ornament was attached to the sinew at his neck, both his clothes and the ornament could have been stolen from him.

Some authors have suggested that the injuries inflicted on Lindow Man had a religious significance and that he was the victim of ritual sacrifice: an offering made to the gods, perhaps carried out by the druids. Because of possible associations between mistletoe and Iron Age religion, the presence of mistletoe pollen in Lindow Man's gut is used to

23 A knotted animal sinew around Lindow Man's neck.

support this argument. It has been suggested that he consumed mistletoe as part of a sacrificial meal or special potion before the sacrifice took place.

Anne Ross, an expert on Iron Age religion, thought that Lindow Man suffered a 'triple death': he was hit on the head, strangled and had his throat cut. It could be argued that he was also 'drowned' when placed face down in a pool in the bog. These different 'deaths' can be related to various gods mentioned in classical and medieval Irish and Welsh texts, indicating that Lindow Man was offered as a sacrifice to these different gods.

The idea that Lindow Man was sacrificed may seem far-fetched; however, it becomes easier to understand when it is set against evidence from bog bodies found elsewhere in northern Europe and the history of archaeological investigation of bog bodies. Bog bodies first came to widespread public attention in 1965 with the publication of the classic book *The Bog People* by the Danish archaeologist Peter Vilhelm Glob. This beautifully

24 The head of Tollund Man, discovered in 1950 in Bjaeldskovdal Mose, Central Jutland, Denmark. He was around thirty years old when he died and was found with a noose around his neck. In 1987 Silkeborg Museum, where Tollund Man is displayed, made a replica of his body as, unlike his head, it was not preserved.

written book has been very influential in interpreting subsequent finds of bog bodies. It details the discoveries of two Danish bog bodies, Tollund Man and Grauballe Man, comparing them to other bodies found in bogs in Denmark and elsewhere in Europe. Glob noticed that many bog bodies had suffered violent deaths (see the table opposite). As already noted, Grauballe Man's throat was cut from ear to ear. Tollund Man was found with a noose around his neck. Similarities can also be drawn between other bog bodies. Many were deposited naked. Some were deliberately submerged in pools of water, tied down by withies (willow sticks) or buried under reeds. Glob showed that bodies were placed in bogs on purpose. He knew that water was significant to the beliefs of Iron Age people and, drawing on the descriptions of Iron Age societies by Roman writers such as Tacitus, Glob suggested that these people were the victims of ritual sacrifice and were deposited in bogs as offerings to the gods. They may have gone willingly to their deaths, or perhaps were criminals or prisoners of war.

The causes of death of some well-known bog bodies

Name	Location of discovery	Date	Cause of death
Borremose Man	1946, Borremose, Himmerland, Denmark	8th century BC	Strangled
Clonycavan Man	2003, near Clonycavan, Ireland	–	Blow to the head
Dätgen Man	1959, Grosses Moor, northern Germany	150 BC	Stabbed in chest and decapitated
Elling Girl	1938, Bjaeldskovdal Mose, Central Jutland, Denmark	200 BC	Hanging
Gallagh Man	1821, County Gallagh, Ireland	1st century BC	Strangled
Old Croghan Man	2003, near Croghan, Ireland	–	Decapitated, stab wounds, broken ribs
Roum Mose Girl	1942, Roum Mose, Himmerland, Denmark	Iron Age	Decapitated
Tollund Man	1950, Bjaeldskovdal Mose, Central Jutland, Denmark	375 BC	Hanging
Two men from Weerdinger	1904, Bourtangermoor, The Netherlands	160 BC–AD 220	One man had a stab wound to the heart
Windeby Man	1952, Schleswig-Holstein, Germany	–	Strangled
Worsley Man	1959, Worsley Moss, Lancashire, England	Roman period	Heavy blows to the head, cord around neck, decapitated
Yde Girl	1897, Drenthe, The Netherlands	1st century AD	Strangled

Questioning sacrifice

The interpretation that Lindow Man was killed as a sacrifice to the gods was questioned by the historian Ronald Hutton in 2004. Hutton demonstrated that alternative theories to sacrifice cannot be excluded using the evidence currently available. The belief that Lindow Man was sacrificed is heavily reliant on Iain West's account of how Lindow Man died but, as we have seen, Robert Connolly's alternative version of the events leading to Lindow Man's death raises significant doubts over the cause of some of the injuries highlighted by West.

Hutton also raised another important question, which is critical to our understanding of why Lindow Man was killed: when exactly did he die? The majority of existing interpretations presume he died in the Iron Age. As explained in the second chapter of this book, Lindow Man probably died some time in the first century AD. What has not been established is whether he died during the Iron Age period or after the Roman conquest of this part of Britain some time in the early AD 60s. We also do not know if he was a native to the region, a stranger or even a Roman. This information is critical in interpreting the evidence because if he was an outsider it is less likely that he went willingly to his death as a sacrifice to the gods. If he was a Roman then he may have been a captured prisoner, taken in conflict during the Romans' occupation of the region. Alternatively, it could indicate that Lindow Man died during the Roman period and not the Iron Age.

The interpretation that Lindow Man was sacrificed situates the context of his death alongside European bog bodies. As we have seen, bog bodies are found over an extended period of time and across a wide geographical area and, although practices may be related, there can be no single explanation as to why people were placed in bogs. Rather than putting forward a generalized explanation it is more appropriate to examine the motivations behind the phenomenon on a case-by-case basis and over smaller geographical areas. For example, Eamonn Kelly, at the National Museum of Ireland, has noticed that many Irish bog bodies are located close to ancient land boundaries, suggesting perhaps that the bodies served a protective function.

The death of Lindow Man did not occur in isolation. At least two other bog bodies were deposited at Lindow Moss and another, Worsley Man, was found only 20 kilometres away. As Worsley Man and the other bog bodies found at Lindow Moss are securely Roman in date, it could be argued that Lindow Man probably died in the Roman period. At least one of these bodies shows signs of 'overkill': Worsley Man received heavy blows to the head and there was a cord around his neck. He was also decapitated. Unfortunately the remains of the other two bog bodies from Lindow Moss are not sufficiently intact to determine whether they also suffered violent deaths, but as only the skull of Lindow Woman has been recovered and the head of Lindow III is also missing, this may indicate that they were also decapitated.

Why was he killed?

Following the evidence laid out in this chapter, are we any closer to establishing why Lindow Man suffered such a violent death and was deposited in a pool at Lindow Moss? He may have been a willing or hesitant human sacrifice or offering made to the gods; an executed criminal; the victim of a violent crime; a member of the community, or an outsider, or even a Roman. However, it is possible to suggest that some of these different explanations of why he died are more or less likely than others.

The argument that Lindow Man was robbed and murdered does not satisfactorily explain the circumstances of his death. Motivations for robbery are difficult to establish. There is no clear evidence that the animal sinew secured an ornament. Since other naked bog bodies have also been discovered, his clothes were probably removed as part of the events leading to his death rather than being stolen after he was killed. The injuries inflicted on Lindow Man were also far more severe than was necessary to murder and rob him. Other bodies have also been discovered at Lindow and Worsley Mosses, indicating that it was no accident that Lindow Man's body was placed face down in a pool in Lindow Moss, far away from evident settlements.

25 Lindow Man's face, showing his furrowed brow and beard.

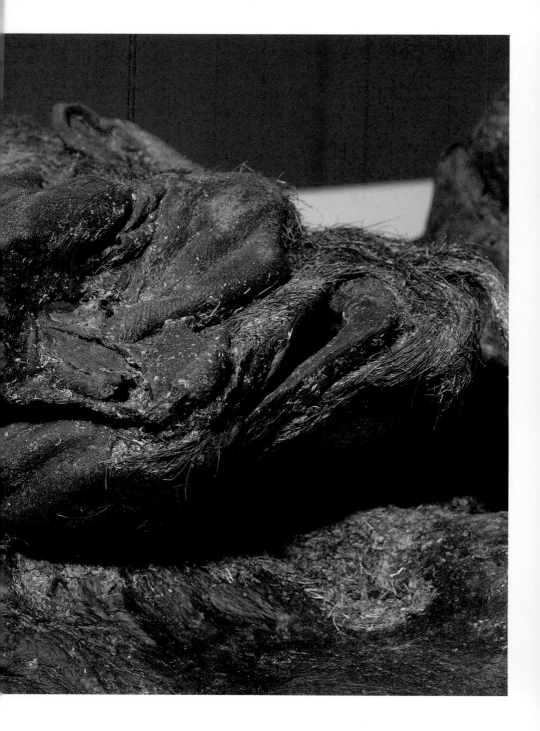

The interpretation that Lindow Man was sacrificed fits the evidence better, but again raises problems. The idea that he suffered a 'triple death' cannot be proven as three separate deaths cannot be satisfactorily identified from his injuries. However, this does not exclude the possibility that he was sacrificed or killed in a special way as far more violence was used than was required to kill him.

On current evidence, as the other bodies from Lindow Moss are dated to the Roman period, Lindow Man is likely to have been killed after the Roman occupation of north-west England. Although his death could have resulted from practices established in the Iron Age period, if he died after the Roman occupation it becomes more difficult to compare his death to that of other Iron Age bog bodies, many of which occurred up to four hundred years earlier. If Lindow Man died in the Roman period it is less likely that he was a sacrifice to the gods, but the possibility cannot be completely excluded. Human sacrifice was prohibited under Roman law. However, this does not mean that it did not happen or that other forms of ritualized killing did not take place in Roman Britain. Even today in countries where capital punishment is legal the execution of prisoners is highly ritualized. Prisoners are given a last meal, and a priest may deliver the last rites.

In the region at the time of Lindow Man's death there was a tradition of placing bodies in bogs. At least two of these people suffered violent deaths. It is impossible to be certain exactly why Lindow Man was killed. He may have been a criminal or a prisoner. He may even have gone to his death as a willing sacrifice. His body was placed in the bog because it was significant to the religious beliefs of people in the region. It was also important that his death was violent. His death may appear brutal but it should be judged from the perspective of the beliefs of people at the time.

Life and death
Lindow Man was a healthy man in the prime of life. He suffered from a mild case of parasitic worms and was developing arthritis in his lower back. He took care over his appearance, trimming his hair and beard and filing his

nails. His face was full of character with a furrowed brow and small ears. He was well muscled, indicating that he was well fed. The condition of his nails and lack of calluses on his hands show that he probably led a relatively privileged life and may have been a figure of some social standing. Certainly in the months before he died he had not performed significant levels of hard, physical work. Then one day in his mid-twenties, some time after a meal of bread, he was violently killed and his body was placed face down in a pool in Lindow Moss.

Lindow Man's death raises many more questions than answers. In the future new dating techniques and methods of refining existing dates could confirm whether Lindow Man died before or after the Roman occupation of northern England. Further scientific developments may mean that it will be possible not only to determine what he ate for his last meal but his diet in the months leading up to his death through analysis of his hair. If he were shown to have had a special diet in the months before he died, this may tip the balance back in favour of the interpretation that Lindow Man was sacrificed. Evidence of the environment in which a person grew up, such as climate or geology, can also be uncovered from analysis of tooth enamel. Future analysis of Lindow Man's teeth may establish whether he grew up in north-west England or somewhere else.

The story of Lindow Man, his death and the details we have so far been able to reconstruct about his life are compelling and trigger genuine fascination in visitors to the British Museum. His remains are especially thought-provoking as, unlike a skeleton, he is fleshed, with visible human features. With the help of the reconstruction of his face, which is full of character with a deeply furrowed brow and small ears, it is possible to imagine how he may have looked as a human being. Many visitors comment on the fact that he looks no different from people today. As I hope has been demonstrated throughout this short book, there are still many unanswered questions and it is desirable that, as new scientific techniques are developed, we can unravel some of the mysteries still surrounding Lindow Man.

26 Between April 2008 and April 2009 Lindow Man was loaned to the Manchester Museum for the third time as part of the British Museum's Partnership UK scheme. Here Jim Peters and Haneesha Melwani discuss how best to pack Lindow Man prior to the loan.

27 Preparing to move Lindow Man to Manchester.

Further reading

Although now out of print, the most comprehensive account of Lindow Man, his discovery, conservation and the scientific research carried out on his body is *Lindow Man: the Body in the Bog* by I.M. Stead, J.B. Bourke and D. Brothwell, published in 1986 by British Museum Publications. *Bog Bodies: new discoveries and new perspectives* by R. Turner and R. Scaife, published in 1995 by the British Museum Press, contains an account of later finds from Lindow Moss, as well as further scientific research on Lindow Man. Other sources that may be of interest are listed below.

Asingh, P., and Lynnerup, N. (eds), *Grauballe Man: An Iron Age Bog Body Revisited*, Moesgård, 2007

Brothwell, D., *The Bog Man and the Archaeology of People*, London, 1986

Connolly, R.C., 'Lindow Man – a prehistoric bog corpse', *Anthropology Today* 1(5) (1985), pp. 15–17

Cowell, A.P., 'The Lindow Man', *Photographic Journal* (March 1985)

Glob, P.V., *The Bog People: Iron-Age Man Preserved*, New York, 1965

Gowlett, J.A.J., Hedges, R.E.M., and Law, I.A., 'Radiocarbon accelerator (AMS) dating of Lindow Man', *Antiquity* 63 (1989), pp. 71–9

Hill, J.D., 'Lindow Man's moustache – another version of death in the peat bog', *Times Literary Supplement* (2004)

Hutton, R., 'What did happen to Lindow Man?', *Times Literary Supplement* (January 2004)

Kelly, E.P., *Kingship and sacrifice: Iron Age bog bodies and boundaries* (Archaeology Ireland Heritage Guide no. 35, 2006)

Omar, S., McCord, M., and Daniels, V., 'The Conservation of Bog Bodies by Freeze-Drying', *Studies in Conservation* (1989), pp. 101–9

Parker-Pearson, M., 'Lindow Man and the Danish connection: Further light on the Mystery of the Bogman', *Anthropology Today* 2(1) (1986), pp. 15–18

Van der Sanden, W., *Through Nature to Eternity: the bog bodies of northwest Europe*, Amsterdam, 1996

1 Photo courtesy of Bryan Sitch
2 Photo courtesy of Rick Turner
3 Map drawn by Stephen Crummy
4 Photo courtesy of Rick Turner
5 Photo: British Museum
6 © Sunday Telegraph
8 Photo: British Museum
9 Photo: British Museum; P&E 1984,1002.1
12 Photo courtesy of Cheshire County Constabulary
13 Photo: British Museum; P&E 1857,0715.1
14 Photo courtesy of the Royal Marsden Hospital
15 Photo courtesy of the Royal Marsden Hospital
16 Photo courtesy of St Bartholomew's Hospital
19 Photo: British Museum
20 Photo: British Museum
21 Photo by Robert Clark, repr. courtesy of Moesgård Museum
22 Photo: British Museum
23 Photo: British Museum
24 Photo courtesy of Silkeborg Museum
25 Photo: British Museum
26 Photo: British Museum
27 Photo: British Museum